50 THINGS YOU DIDN'T KNOW ABOUT

Colonial America

Written and Illustrated
by Sean O'Neill

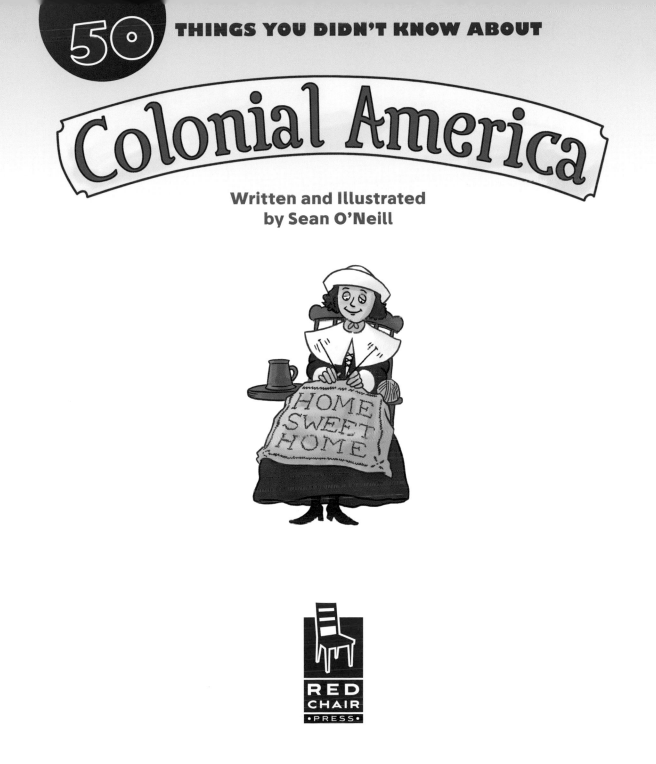

RED
CHAIR
·PRESS·

50 Things You Didn't Know About is produced and published by Red Chair Press:
www.redchairpress.com

Publisher's Cataloging-In-Publication Data

Names: O'Neill, Sean, 1968- author, illustrator.

Title: 50 things you didn't know about. Colonial America / written and illustrated by Sean O'Neill.

Other Titles: 50 things you didn't know about colonial America | Fifty things you didn't know about colonial America | Colonial America

Description: [South Egremont, Massachusetts] : Red Chair Press, [2020] | Series: 50 things you didn't know about | Interest age level: 007-010. | Includes bibliographical references and index. | Summary: "Toothless at twenty in Colonial America? Discover some of the most amazing and amusing facts about life in Colonial America and how the Pilgrims survived it all."--Provided by publisher.

Identifiers: ISBN 9781634407960 (library hardcover) | ISBN 9781634408080 (ebook)

Subjects: LCSH: United States--Civilization--To 1783--Juvenile literature. | United States--Social life and customs--To 1775--Juvenile literature. | CYAC: United States--Civilization--To 1783. | United States--Social life and customs--To 1775.

Classification: LCC E162 .O54 2020 (print) | LCC E162 (ebook) | DDC 973.2 [E]--dc23

LCCN: 2019931712

Printed in the United States of America

0819 1P CGS20

TABLE of CONTENTS

THE NEW WORLD

European explorers began sailing across the Atlantic Ocean in the 15th and 16th centuries in hopes of finding a new trading route to Asia. What they found instead were two continents filled with many strange new discoveries. Of course, many thousands of Native peoples had been living in the Americas for centuries, but to the many European settlers that began traveling across the sea in search of a new home, this was, truly, a "new world."

1. Although we give credit to Columbus for discovering the "new world," he himself didn't believe it. After four voyages across the Atlantic, he still thought he had found a new route to Asia.

2. Christopher Columbus wasn't the first European to reach North America. In 1001 C.E. a group of Scandinavian sailors led by Leif Ericson landed in what is now Eastern Canada. Among the discoveries they made was a plant they had never seen—grapevines. Because of this, they named the new land Vinland.

YOU ARE NOW LEAVING
VINLAND
THANKS FOR VISITING!

5

3 North and South America were named after Italian explorer Amerigo Vespucci. His exploration of the South American coast in 1501 convinced most people (but not Columbus!) that this was a new land, not part of Asia.

4 The English weren't the only ones to establish colonies in the Americas. The Spanish had colonies in Mexico, Florida, and California, and there were several French, Dutch, and Swedish colonies as well.

5 Most explorers were hoping to find gold in the New World. Many ships were sent back to Europe full of a type of shiny rock called *pyrite*—also known as *fool's gold*.

6 The **colony** of Pennsylvania was founded by William Penn, who established it as a home for members of the Quaker religion.

7 The colony of Georgia was settled by a group of English colonists that owed large debts that they couldn't repay. These debtors were sent to Georgia to raise silk worms and send silk back to England to repay their debt.

8 Europeans discovered many new foods in the New World that didn't exist in Europe, including corn (maize), squash, pumpkin, avocado, and chocolate!

ABOARD THE MAYFLOWER

There may be no more familiar image of the colonial beginnings of this country than the brave group of English Puritans that we call The Pilgrims setting forth into the unknown aboard the *Mayflower*. But some of these facts about the ocean voyage aboard the famous ship may surprise you.

9 There were 102 passengers aboard the *Mayflower*, but only 50 of them were Pilgrims. The rest were crew and other travelers. There were also 2 dogs, some cats, and numerous goats, pigs, and chickens.

10 The *Mayflower* was small and cramped. Passengers had to spend most of the trip in the between-decks area, which was only 5 feet (1.5 m) tall, and stacked to the ceiling with chests, furniture, clothes, linens, and various other supplies.

11 The *Mayflower* stunk! In addition to all those animals, none of the passengers bathed or changed clothes for 66 days! And everyone on board went to the toilet in a bucket and dumped it overboard.

9

12 On long ocean voyages in the 16th and 17th centuries, a little bit of food had to last a long time. One common provision was something called *hardtack*, which was a dry biscuit that would stay edible for months.

IT'S NOT SO BAD IF YOU DIP IT IN THE STEWED PRUNES.

13 Because it was such a long journey and there was little storage space, food aboard the *Mayflower* was pretty limited. In addition to hardtack, the choices were dried pea soup, salted dried fish, or stewed prunes. Yum!

14 One child was born aboard the *Mayflower* during the crossing of the Atlantic. His parents named him Oceanus!

15 Oceanus wasn't the only Pilgrim child with an unusual name. Puritans often named their children after traits that were thought to be important. Some common names included Remember, Humility, Patience, Charity, and Unity.

16 One clever colonist named William Mullins brought 126 pairs of shoes and 13 pairs of boots to sell to settlers once he arrived in America.

PILGRIMS OF PLYMOUTH

The settlers that survived the crossing aboard the *Mayflower* didn't have long to recover from the trip. They quickly set up a town, which they called *Plymouth Plantation*, and had to get right to work. Winter would be coming soon, so they wasted no time building shelters, figuring out how to grow food in this new land, and getting to know the new neighbors!

WATCH YOUR STEP, MA'AM.

PLYMOUTH ROCK

17 Pilgrims aboard the *Mayflower* didn't actually land at Plymouth, although they did settle there eventually. Their first stop in the new world was actually Cape Cod on the Massachusetts coast.

18 There is a real Plymouth Rock, but nobody knows if the Pilgrims actually stepped on it when they went ashore. The rock was never mentioned until 121 years after the Pilgrims arrived.

19 The Pilgrims also befriended a Native American named Squanto, who not only spoke English; he had actually been to England!

20 The first Native American visitor to Plymouth was an Algonkian named Samoset. The pilgrims were surprised when he spoke perfect English! As it turned out, he had met some English explorers and fishermen a few years before who taught him English.

21 Native North Americans taught the English settlers many tricks about farming, including how to place a dead fish into the ground with the seeds to act as fertilizer.

22 The first year at Plymouth was rough, and more than half the pilgrims died over the winter. The dead were buried at night in unmarked graves because they were afraid the Native Americans would attack if they knew how few of them were left.

23 The Pilgrims and Native Americans got along well for a while, but the good times didn't last. In 1675 war broke out between the Wampanoag tribe and the English settlers.

24 In colonial times, a bed was made with several pieces of rope stretched across a bed frame, which the mattress was then set onto. Over time, the ropes would sag and need to be tightened. That's why we say "sleep tight" before bed!

25 The first Thanksgiving wasn't really Thanksgiving, and it wasn't really the first. What we today call "Thanksgiving" was actually a harvest festival, and these had been held by Native North Americans for many years before the Pilgrims arrived.

26 Pilgrims didn't actually wear buckles on their hats and shoes. That was something that was made up by artists later. Metal would have been much too hard to come by to make a buckle for your hat!

WHY IS YOUR HAT WEARING A BELT?

27 The Puritan settlers of Massachusetts started Cambridge College (later called Harvard) just six years after they landed. Each member of the colony paid the college twelve **pence** and a peck of corn a year. Tuition's gone up a little since then!

28 Many more Pilgrims came to the colonies in the 1600s, but some of them went back home. When the English Civil War broke out in 1642, many English Puritans returned to England to fight against the king.

CHAPTER 4

DAILY LIFE

Life in the colonies wasn't easy. Settlers that traveled to the New World left behind many comforts of home back in Europe and had to learn to make do with what they could find, what they could make, and what they could grow. But the colonists were very resourceful, and over time, began to make a life for themselves. Many of these facts about how the colonists lived may surprise you.

29 The first homes built by colonial settlers were simple structures made of tree saplings and grass. Because of their resemblance to the Native North Americans' homes, they were called *English wigwams*.

30 The first log cabins in the colonies were built by Swedish colonists in a settlement called Fort Christina (in today's Delaware). The Swedes knew how to keep warm, and this style of house was soon copied throughout the colonies.

I THINK THOSE SWEDES ARE ON TO SOMETHING!

31 Most towns and villages in the colonies were **democratic**. *Everyone* had a vote—as long as you were a man, owned land, and belonged to a church!

32 Because china and metal were scarce and expensive, dishes, like many things, were made out of wood. Early colonists ate their meals off of a *trencher*, which was a piece of wood with a hollow spot carved out of the center.

33 It was necessary to keep a fire burning in the home at all times, for heat and for cooking. If it ever went out, a child was sent to a neighbor's with a fire scoop to get a few hot coals. Otherwise, re-lighting the fire with a *tinder* could take a half hour.

34 In autumn, groups would go out into the forest to gather nuts that had fallen to the ground from wind and rain. These outings were called *nutting parties*.

35 In colonial towns, people threw their garbage into the streets, and at night, pigs were let loose to eat it all.

36 Colonists had to make their own home remedies when they were sick. One remedy for a nagging cough was to boil snail shells with earthworms and drink it with milk. Yuk!

37 Dental hygiene was not a priority. Colonists used salt, sand, or ground-up bricks to clean their teeth. But most people were toothless by age twenty, although they blamed it on drinking tea and eating warm bread.

I TOLD YOU TO LAY OFF THE WARM BREAD!

I CAN'T HELP MYSELF.

38 Before becoming father of our country, thirteen-year-old George Washington wrote "Rules of Civility and Decent Behavior in Company." One rule: "In the presence of others, sing not to yourself, nor drum with your fingers or feet."

39 Colonists who traded with Native Americans began to use the Native's form of money, called *wampum*. Wampum was strings of beads made from shells. Purple shells were worth the most.

40 Children were expected to help out with the household chores, and there was a lot to be done. Children churned butter, hulled corn, and shelled nuts.

41 At mealtime adults sat in chairs, but children were made to stand and eat what was served to them in complete silence.

42 Colonial children wore loose gowns until the age of five. On their fifth birthday they received their first pair of breeches (pants) and their very first pair of shoes!

YOU'LL NEVER GUESS WHAT IT IS!

43 Children didn't have much in the way of toys and games, but they made do with what they could find. One popular activity was to roll a metal hoop from a barrel while running. Another popular game was Hide the Thimble. Sound like fun?

44 If families wanted toys for their children, they had to make their own. Many colonial children played with dolls made from dried cornhusks.

45 Fresh water was hard to come by so most people, including children, drank beer or ale. In the 1600s a "morning draft" of beer or hard cider was common before breakfast!

46 Colonial women generally wore a hood, or bonnet, on their heads. A woman who had lost her husband wore a cap with a small point in front. That's where we get the term "widow's peak."

47 Punishment for crimes was based on public humiliation. People found guilty of minor crimes were locked in the stocks or the **pillory**, and a letter indicating their crime was hung around their neck: "D" for drunkenness or "B" for blasphemy.

48 Dutch colonists brought an amazing innovation to America from Holland—the waffle iron! They also enjoyed sweet cakes and doughnuts fried in fat.

49 We can thank the Dutch for some of our favorite winter sports. They are responsible for bringing ice skates to America, and they invented downhill sledding!

50 The Dutch lived in a colony they called New Netherland, and they called the main town New Amsterdam. If you've never heard of it that's because when the English moved in, they changed the name—to New York!

Glossary

colony: a new and distant place under control of another nation

democratic: intending to be socially equal

pence: a coin equal to a penny

pillory: a wooden frame that can lock the head and hands, used in public shaming.

Explore Colonial America More

Books

Cook, Peter. *You Wouldn't Want to Sail on the Mayflower!* Franklin Watts, 2013.

Mara, Wil. *If You Were a Kid in the Thirteen Colonies.* Children's Press, 2016.

Raum, Elizabeth. *The Scoop on Clothes, Homes, and Daily Life in Colonial America.* Capstone Press, 2017.

Raum, Elizabeth. *The Dreadful, Smelly Colonies.* Capstone Press, 2010.

Index

About the Author/Illustrator

Sean O'Neill is an illustrator and writer living in Chicago. He is the creator of the *Rocket Robinson* series of graphic novels. Sean loves history, trivia, and drawing cartoons, so this project is pretty much a dream assignment. Plus, it comes with breakfast ale and waffles!